I0060716

S.M.A.R.T. Goals
For Christian Entrepreneurs

A Guide to Achieving Success in ALL areas of Life

Trista Laborn

Trista Laborn

S.M.A.R.T. Goals For Christian Entrepreneurs
A Guide to Achieving Success in ALL Areas of Life

Although the author and publisher have made every effort to ensure that the information in this book was correct at press time, the author and publisher (Trista Laborn & DiViNE Purpose Publishing) do not assume and hereby disclaim any liability to any party for any loss, damage, or disruption caused by errors or omissions, whether such errors or omissions result from negligence, accident, or any other cause.

This publication contains the opinions and ideas of its author. Relevant laws vary from state to state. The strategies outlined in this book may not be suitable for every individual, and are not guaranteed or warranted to produce any particular results.

No warranty is made with respect to the accuracy or completeness of the information contained herein, and both the author and publisher specifically disclaim any responsibility for any liability, loss, or risk, personal or otherwise, which is incurred as a consequence, directly or indirectly, of the use and application of any of the contents of this book.

This book or parts thereof may not be reproduced in any form, stored in a retrieval system, or transmitted in any form by any means—electronic, mechanical, photocopy, recording, or otherwise—without prior written permission of the publisher/author, except as provided by United States of America copyright law.

Scripture taken from the Holy Bible, NEW INTERNATIONAL VERSION®, NIV® Copyright © 1973, 1978, 1984, 2011 by Biblica, Inc.® Used by permission. All rights reserved worldwide.

"Scripture quotations taken from the Amplified® Bible, Copyright © 1954, 1958, 1962, 1964, 1965, 1987 by The Lockman Foundation Used by permission." (www.Lockman.org)

Published by Divine Purpose Publishing
www.divinepurposepublishing.com
P.O. Box 906
Branford, CT. 06405
(866) 211-7637

Copyright © 2015 Trista Laborn

All rights reserved.
ISBN-13: 978-0692485408
ISBN-10: 0692485406
LCCN: 2015945900
Printed in the United States of America

DEDICATION

S. M. A. R. T. Goals for the Christian entrepreneur is dedicated to those looking to live the life God has in store for you (Jeremiah 29:11).

This book is also dedicated to my three children, Layla, Aaron and Olivia. You guys were my motivation for starting this book. When you follow God's way, you will see that He has a way of giving you the kind of life that you would've never asked for or imagined having (Ephesians 3:20).

ACKNOWLEDGEMENTS

I thank my husband, Enel Laborn, for helping and supporting me throughout this journey. For believing in me as I walk this out. You are an AMAZING man of God and I love you so much.

I want to thank my family and friends for supporting and encouraging me along the way. And a special thank you to Rebecca Garcia, for pushing me out of my comfort zone, mentoring and helping me to pursue my God-given dream.

I want to thank my Father in heaven for looking after me and walking beside me through this journey of being a Christian entrepreneur.

Table of Contents

Introduction   6
Chapter 1: How it All Started   10

Chapter 2: The Fundamentals of Having
a Successful Business   19

Chapter 3: The Call   21
 Luke 5:1-11 (Simon Peter's new job title)

Chapter 4: Stepping Out   29
Matthew 14:22-33 (Peter stepping out into the deep)

Chapter 5: Faith Walk   37
Genesis 37 & 39; 41:1-49 (Trusting God in the process)

Chapter 6: S.M.A.R.T. Goals   45
(The practical guide to Godly success in all areas of
your life)

    -Seek (Find Him for the answers)

    -Meditate (What's in your heart)

    -Armor (Staying equipped for success)

    -Run (Run and press toward the goal to win the prize)

    -Transformation (The heart transplant)

Conclusion   74
Scriptures for Motivation   76

Introduction

I'm a wife, mom of three and an entrepreneur. I'm pouring from my heart the journey of where God has taken me. He has taken me from a shy, little girl to a BOLD, beautiful woman after God's own heart.

This book is not intended for me to preach at you or tell you what to do. I just want to share my heart and my journey with you. I am not saying that my journey is finished, because I know God is still leading me in the direction I should go in regards to my marriage, being a mother and entrepreneur.

This book was birthed at a time in my life where I struggled with trying to balance all of the roles God had blessed me to undertake. I desperately wanted to do what God had called me to do so that I could make a difference. I wanted to share with others the night and day difference He had made in my life (1 Peter 2:9). And, of course, make money to help support my family. I wanted it so much, that I realized I had begun to hustle and grind in the marketplace. I was working so hard doing whatever it took to build my business, all the while hurting my family in the process.

My home life was suffering. I wasn't giving

my family the attention they needed and deserved at the time. I didn't know how to run my household AND a business. My husband began to share with me how he had been feeling. He felt like I didn't care about him anymore and that my feelings for him had changed because so much of my energy was going towards the business God had given me.

I felt like a failure because my marriage was suffering. What was I doing wrong? Maybe I wasn't planning and scheduling my time correctly. Maybe I'm not supposed to be in business. Or just maybe, I had never heard from God from the start. But what I had learned, was that in order to be successful in anything I did, I must first seek God. God was ALWAYS cultivating a heart for Him in me. I began seeking after HIM, HIS face and not HIS hands. I want to share this story with other women that have gone through the same struggles as I did. I'm here to tell you that God is more concerned about your heart than He is about the amount of money in your bank account.

Trying to "balance" it all is not realistic. The word balance in the dictionary means, *"The state of having your weight spread equally so that you do not fall."* I was trying to do just that. I was trying to give equal time to each area of my life, as a wife, mom, entrepreneur, housekeeper, and then trying to take care of myself. After a while, I was tired. It didn't seem realistic to me. The problem with "spreading your weight equally" is that you will eventually fall. I couldn't give myself equally to the different demands on my life and still run a successful business.

I HAD to seek God's face for the answer on how to do this. I knew without a shadow of doubt He called me to build this business, and to handle the demands of my everyday life.

Now... I no longer, fight for time to spend with my family, or time to even run my business. In fact, I'm able to spend time with my husband, my three children and still successfully make money in my business, because I have given EVERYTHING I am to God and have allowed Him to direct my steps EVERYDAY.

In this book, I have written the step-by-step course God has taken me through to be successful in all areas of life. I will also share stories from the Bible, examples of what can happen if you follow God's principles for success. And as you begin to study and meditate on the scriptures and stories given, you will begin to understand that God wants us to succeed more than we do.

I have structured this book to have certain points where there is an action plan noted, and a place for your note-taking. It is important to write down any thoughts, feelings or directions that God will be speaking to your spirit as you take this journey (Jeremiah 30:2). I have also included note-summaries in some sections to help bring the point of the passage altogether.

CHAPTER ONE

How It All Started...

In 2009, I was playing with the idea of getting my haircut to start growing locs and beginning other things, because I really believed that God was doing new things in my life. And even though I was working a full-time job, I began doing research and learning about the use of natural ingredients for my hair and body.

I felt the desire so strongly to start a business, but didn't know exactly what I wanted to do. I was heavy in church activities, so I began to ask questions and see what others were doing as a business. Then I began to **seek** God for the answer. I felt and told God, "I know you are calling me to start a business and I will do it because I know you will be with me." At the time, I didn't know what that meant. After a while of seeking and asking questions, God told me candles, specifically massage candles. Candles that when lit, will melt into a pool of oil for your skin, which will be made with natural ingredients. I LOVED the idea! I began the research and soon after I started making them. I also knew that God was going to give me other products that I would make naturally, but the start was the candles. After a while, I realized essential oils had an impact in the way a person felt. I wanted people to feel energized, relaxed and happy when using my products. As the journey of getting my business began, I started to meet people. These people poured into me and gave me tips on how to start this business. Things like, what paperwork I needed to have and how to go about advertising. I even began blogging and sharing healthy and all natural tips and recipes.

After **meditating** on the tips that were given to me by the different people I met, I finally came up with a product and name for my business. It was called going to be called, "Trista's Creations." I was set and excited about starting this new adventure, I even named my blog: Trista's Creations.

On my way to the courthouse to get my license and paperwork taken care of, God spoke to me and said, "Not yet. This is not the name of your business." So I said, "Ok God, what is the name?" He didn't give me the name until 3 days later. I was at work (I was working at a childcare center at the time) and while I was cleaning, God dropped it in my spirit: Silk Spa Creations. I LOVED it and was SUPER excited that I finally got the name of my business and I literally ran to the courthouse to get the paperwork so I could get started. Now that I had my paperwork together, I began to market and sell my candles. I began to do parties to showcase to people how the candles worked and how the candle oils turned into sugar scrubs to use as a body treatment. I eventually started getting my candles in spas around the area, while at the same time still working full time. It was beginning to get overwhelming. I felt like if I got up, prayed, and put on the **armor** of God to fight my way through the demands of my life while still building my business that it would all pay off. But, at the time, I had young school age children and my husband was starting to feel like I wasn't taking the family serious. The money I was making at my job and business, I was being put back into my business and not into my household and my husband had a problem with that. He wanted to see the business flourish and so did I, but I wasn't doing it the right way. It was difficult because I felt that working the way I was working, was the only way to do it. My business was in its beginning stages so it took a lot of time and effort to get it started, and because of that my family suffered. It became too hard to see my family hurting and I was starting to feel like maybe I didn't hear from God or maybe it wasn't the right time, etc. So, with all the frustration and overwhelming feelings I was having I decided to let go of the business. I felt like it wasn't benefitting me and my family. I felt like I should just stop and so I did. When trials and storms came to discourage me while I was in the process, I ran the other way. I couldn't see how my business would flourish, so I ran in the opposite direction.

During this time, my husband got orders to be relocated in California. I felt like this was a perfect time to start over and begin anew. When we got to California, I felt a strong urge once again to start a business. So I got involved with a few companies, one of them being Scentsy. I loved the products and was doing pretty good in the business. One day, while speaking with a lady friend, she had mentioned to me that I shouldn't be doing Scentsy and that I needed to get back to building my Silk Spa Creations business.

I felt like this was God telling me to stop and get back to my building my business. She began to pray for me and the fire to start again lit up so bright and hot in me, that I went running again with my business. Even with everything that had happened before with my husband and the demands of my lifestyle, I felt like, now I can handle it because again, God has called me to it. He would see me through it. I began to do the process again to build my business. I started working late hours, spending money we didn't have, and going to events to network to get my business out there. Now, in California there are a lot more opportunities and events to showcase your products. All of sudden I started feeling overwhelmed again. I was at a low point. It was at this point when my husband began to tell me he felt like I didn't care about him. And once again, I felt like a failure and wanted to quit. The whole point of me even doing this business was to help support my family. Where was I going wrong?

At this time, God was beginning a new thing in my heart. A **transformation** that was more for Him than in making money. He began to show me that I was following the rules of the world and not Him. Even though I started with Him, it was like I took hold of the business and ran with it, instead of allowing God to lead it and be CEO of it. I want to share my story with you because you may be trying to start your own business and are feeling the same feelings I felt in the beginning. But I am here to let you know that God has a better plan for you and wants to see you succeed in business as much as you do. (Jeremiah 29:11).

Before I get started with the fundamentals, let me share with you that serving God made a big impact on my business growth. This was how I began the process of getting my business started. God began to show me that I was not consistent in the things He called me to do. At the time, I was singing on the praise team, I was writing a few blog posts on, "A Purpose Driven

Wife", formerly known as, "Trista's Creations," and ultimately and most importantly, I wasn't giving my family the time they needed from me. Even though I was being pulled in different directions, I gave my attention to my business and left everything else. So, I had to stop and wait for direction from God concerning my business.

In my waiting, my daughter was having an EXTREMELY difficult time. She was dealing with self-esteem issues due to her hair and she was having difficulty with math. These things caused a lot of issues with her confidence. She also started acting out in school. So much so, that they were going to fail her in the 4th grade for not participating in class. She did not participate because she felt it was too hard for her. I'm not as good in math as my husband is, but he couldn't help her because he had been working late hours and then, eventually, he was deployed. I felt my daughter was too smart to fail the 4th grade. I felt helpless. I really sought after God for help because I didn't know what to do. I began to really dig into my daughter's homework and help her with her math as best as I could. The teachers were VERY understanding and helped A LOT. One day, I shared with my woman's study group that I was having a hard time and they suggested praying before helping her with her homework. That WORKED! I went from helping her with homework until midnight, to her not even needing my help. With God's help, I was able to help her with her hair and her homework. She eventually got her confidence back.

While I waited for God's direction, I began to set times for my children. I began to do different things with them such as working out before or after homework, creating family movie nights, creating fun weekend outings, etc. I also had to become more consistent in church. For instance, being faithful and on time for service. I also had to be faithful in my obligations to the praise team. I had to arrive on time to the practices, and not just when I felt like it. It wasn't that I didn't want to, but it was because when I did go, I had to bring my children and make sure that I kept them quiet. I didn't want to go through the hassle. But God showed me that I was willing to do whatever it took for my business and not for the things concerning His house. That was a wakeup call for me.

In essence, I was already using the S.M.A.R.T. goals for Christian entrepreneurs in my Christian lifestyle, but using the tools the world system had to build my business. You can't use the world's system to build your God given business. It doesn't go together.

I began to serve faithfully wherever God was calling me to serve in His house. I was so faithful that I began to do other things and not be moved by my kids' behavior (God literally took care of that). I also began to frequently post on my blog all that God was putting on my heart to share. Slowly, as I began to take care of my household, the church activities and my blog faithfully, God was able to trust me with other projects.

Luke 16:10, *"One who is faithful in very little is also faithful in much, and one who is dishonest in a very little is also dishonest in much."*

True leadership is servanthood, and the greatest leader of all time is Jesus Christ. God showed us in the Bible, that servanthood is an attitude exemplified by Christ in the way He not only served His disciples but the people. At the time, I didn't have a servant attitude, all I wanted to do was make money to help support my family. What I didn't know was that God was cultivating in me a heart for Him and preparing me for ministry as well as business. My business would be a ministry of helping women get back into loving themselves. In the process of selling my products I would be ministering to the women, encouraging and motivating them. As well as, sharing with them the benefits of using a massage candle for their skin. Serving others is the very essence of ministry. This life I live, is to serve God.

Galatians 2:20 says, *"...the life which I now live in the flesh I live by faith in the Son of God, who loved me and gave Himself for me."*

Ephesians 2:10 says, *"For we are God's [own] handiwork (His workmanship), recreated in Christ Jesus, [born anew] that we may do those good works which God predestined (planned beforehand) for us [taking paths which He prepared ahead of time], that we should walk in them [living the good life which He prearranged and made ready for us to live]."* (Amplified Bible)

This scripture tell me, that I am a servant to God. His handiwork, to do good works on earth that He prepared ahead of time. And that He wants me to live a good life. A life that He has arranged for me to live. Not for me to do whatever feels good to me, but to give Him the glory in the life I live by following the paths which He prepared ahead of time.

This was not an overnight transformation. God was working in me. He showed me ways to stay faithful and serve in the areas He has called me to, including my business, and not have my family suffer in the process.

Let me show you, what He showed me...

CHAPTER 2

The Fundamentals of Having a Successful Business

Before I get started with the fundamentals, we have to get started with your heart and mind set. Our character has to line up and be able to handle the task ahead.

Romans 12:2
"Do not conform to the pattern of this world, but be transformed by the renewing of your mind. Then you will be able to test and approve what God's will is—his good, pleasing and perfect will." (New International Version)

Romans 12:2 starts with, _"Do not conform to the pattern of this world."_ The word "world" means how the world operates. Its values, beliefs, etc. We are called to live by what God has to offer, God's values, and how He operates. Which is to enjoy life, and have it in abundance (to the full, John 10:10).

God also calls us to be transformed by the renewing of our minds. The words **"transformed"** and **"renewing"** are verbs. **Transformed** means *to make a thorough or dramatic change in the form, appearance, or character.* As we begin to study and meditate on God's Word, He will begin to change us.

"Renewing" is also an action word. It means to *repeat, an action or statement.* Being transformed and renewed in God's Word is a daily walk. There is no end, until we meet God again. But while we're on earth, we are continually renewing our mind from how the world operates to how God operates.

We are called to be different than the world around us. As Christian entrepreneurs, we cannot adapt to the world's system of what success is. We are under a different system, and throughout this book I will show you how we can operate under the Kingdom system.

CHAPTER 3

The Call: Luke 5:1-11
(Simon Peter's New Job Title)

Luke 5:1-11

On one occasion, while the crowd was pressing in on him to hear the word of God, he was standing by the lake of Gennesaret, and he saw two boats by the lake, but the fishermen had gone out of them and were washing their nets. Getting into one of the boats, which was Simon's, he asked him to put out a little from the land. And he sat down and taught the people from the boat. And when he had finished speaking, he said to Simon, "Put out into the deep and let down your nets for a catch." And Simon answered, "Master, we toiled all night and took nothing! But at your word I will let down the nets." And when they had done this, they enclosed a large number of fish, and their nets were breaking. They signaled to their partners in the other boat to come and help them. And they came and filled both the boats, so that they began to sink. But when Simon Peter saw it, he fell down at Jesus' knees, saying, "Depart from me, for I am a sinful man, O

Lord." For he and all who were with him were astonished at the catch of fish that they had taken, and so also were James and John, sons of Zebedee, who were partners with Simon. And Jesus said to Simon, "Do not be afraid; from now on you will be catching men." And when they had brought their boats to land, they left everything and followed him.

Summary of the story: When Jesus meets up with Simon (also known as Peter) he begins to give Simon instructions. When Simon had finally listened to Jesus' instructions, Simon caught so much fish that the two boats that they filled began to sink. After that, Simon began to worship Jesus. Jesus then gave Simon a new job. Instead of a fisherman that catches fish, He will be Fishers of Men (a fisherman of souls).

Let's unpack this: First, Simon toiled all night trying to catch fish. The word toil means: "Long strenuous fatiguing labor." Simon gave a lot of energy and effort into trying to catch fish and ended up catching nothing.

The idea is that before Simon came into contact with Jesus, his workload was strenuous. Jesus says in Matthew 11:28-30, *"Come to me, all of you who are weary and carry heavy burdens, and I will give you rest. Take my yoke upon you. Let me teach you, because I am humble and gentle at heart, and you will find rest for your souls. For my yoke is easy to bear, and the burden I give you is light."* (New Living Translation)

God is concerned about you, your lifestyle, your household, business and more importantly, your soul. He wants to bless you with rest. There is no need to strain to get your business off the ground. God has an easy way of doing things. So, does this mean I don't have to work? Do I just wait on God to send me customers? NO! There is still work to do.

Which brings me to my second point: The work won't be strenuous. Simon Peter still had to work. Jesus gave him instructions and there was work in following those directions. The instructions were: (1) Go back into the deep, and (2) let down your net. This was still work Simon had to do. Before that Jesus and Simon were on the shore and now Jesus is giving him instructions to GO BACK into the deep water! This don't make sense.

Why would Jesus tell him to go back? Logic says if you don't catch anything in one spot, you go to another spot to catch fish. Simon said, "At your word, I will let down the nets." The difference is this time Jesus said it. He gave instructions. For Simon to go back out to the same spot where he didn't catch any fish before, just because Jesus said to do it again, took a STEP of FAITH. As followers of Jesus Christ, we WALK BY FAITH (2 Corinthians 5:7).Because it was at HIS Word, (the Bible) that makes ALL the difference. By Simon being obedient, He was blessed beyond measure.

Last point, when we're obedient, God grants us supernatural blessings that we can't get on our own. Hustlin' and grindin' might give me a profitable business, but what about my family? And at what cost?

Action Step: Doing things God's way is the BEST thing you can do for yourself, your business, and your family. You gain so much more. Pray and seek God to give you strategic, "out of the box" ways to be profitable in your business.

Notes: Share in the note section what God is showing you in this scripture and write in down.

_____

_____

_____

_____

_____

S.M.A.R.T. Goals For Christian Entrepreneurs

_____

_____

_____

_____

_____

_____

_____

_____

_____

_____

_____

_____

_____

_____

_____

_____

_____

_____

_____

_____

_____

_____

_____

_____

_____

_____

_____

_____

_____

_____

_____

_____

_____

S.M.A.R.T. Goals For Christian Entrepreneurs

_____

_____

_____

_____

_____

_____

_____

_____

_____

_____

_____

_____

_____

_____

_____

_____

Prayer: Father, I am honored, that you saw fit to call me into the marketplace. I desire to do your will/purpose for my life on earth as it is in heaven (Matthew 6:10). Lord, show me strategic ways to be profitable in my business without causing strain or stress on other areas of my life. Show me where I can also get accurate rest to take care of myself so that I can be effective in your plans for my life, in Jesus' name. AMEN!

CHAPTER 4

Stepping Out: Matthew 14:22-33 (Peter Stepping Out into the Deep)

Matthew 14:22-34:

Immediately he made the disciples get into the boat and go before him to the other side, while he dismissed the crowds. And after he had dismissed the crowds, he went up on the mountain by himself to pray. When evening came, he was there alone, but the boat by this time was a long way from the land, beaten by the waves, for the wind was against them. And in the fourth watch of the night he came to them, walking on the sea. But when the disciples saw him walking on the sea, they were terrified, and said, "It is a ghost!" and they cried out in fear. But immediately Jesus spoke to them, saying, "Take heart; it is I. Do not be afraid." And Peter answered him, "Lord, if it is you, command me to come to you on the water." He said, "Come." So Peter got out of the boat and walked on the water and came to Jesus. But when he saw the wind, he was afraid, and beginning to sink he cried out, "Lord, save me." Jesus immediately reached out his hand and took hold of him, saying to him, "O you of little faith, why did you doubt?" And when they got into the boat, the wind ceased. And those in the boat worshiped him, saying, "Truly you are the Son of God." And when they had crossed over, they came to land at Gennesaret.

Summary of the story: During this time, Jesus heard the news about John the Baptist's death, and he had performed the miracle of feeding the five thousand. After that, he sent the disciples on the boat before him, to go to the other side (V. 22). In the meantime, he went up to the mountain by himself to pray. The disciples were a long way from land and was in a storm in the middle of the night. Then they saw Jesus walking on the sea, (afar off). They got scared and Jesus assured them that it was him. Peter saw this and wanted to walk on water as well. He began to ask Jesus to command him to come to him on the water. Jesus did, and Peter walked on water. It wasn't until Peter began to notice the storm around him that he started to drown in the water. Jesus saves him and they eventually make it to the other side.

Let's unpack this: First, when the disciples were in the boat, traveling to go to the other side, there was a storm. When God calls you into starting your own business, expect storms to come. They will come to either strengthen you or they will come to discourage you. When I started my business, I had a lot of things coming against me to discourage me off the path God had for me. Know that even though there is a storm, you will make it to the other side (V.34). Second, when God calls you into the deep (the marketplace), keep your eyes focused on Jesus and not the things around you, if you do, you WILL get discouraged and drown.

I did this when starting my business. I started off focused on the things of God and then I lost sight, got discouraged and eventually let go of my business. God is with you in the deep. Trust that He will take care of you know matter what it may look like. And lastly, Peter stepped out, noticed that the winds were blowing and began to drown. The crazy thing is, the storm was still going when Peter made the decision to step out and walk on water from the beginning.

Peter noticed when he was walking on the water that the winds were blowing. As entrepreneurs we tend to be a lot like Peter. We take risks. We are willing to go out in the deep. We start off on fire to do the things God has called us to do, but then we sometimes lose sight of that and began to sink, drown and cry out to God for help. I am here to prevent you from drowning, and to help you keep your eyes focused on the plan God has for you in your business. By sharing my story, I want to help you to not make the same mistakes I did, but to learn and be victorious in the marketplace.

Action Step: Sometimes the risk is actually believing and trusting God in the deep. When everything in you wants to cry out for help and to get back in the boat, I want to encourage you to TRUST GOD. Take that leap of faith to DO IT and believe that God will never leave you or forsake you (Deuteronomy 31:6).

Notes: Share what area in your business God is calling you to Trust Him in. Write down the risk, how you plan on stepping out, and how it is making you feel to take such a risk. Then give it to God and allow Him to help you in the process.

_____

_____

_____

_____

_____

_____

_____

_____

_____

_____

_____

_____

_____

_____

_____

_____

_____

_____

_____

_____

_____

_____

_____

_____

_____

_____

_____

_____

_____

_____

_____

_____

_____

_____

_____

_____

_____

_____

_____

_____

_____

S.M.A.R.T. Goals For Christian Entrepreneurs

_____

_____

_____

_____

_____

_____

_____

_____

_____

_____

_____

_____

_____

_____

_____

_____

_____

_____

Prayer: Father, help me with my unbelief (Mark 9:24). Help me to truly trust You in the marketplace and not lean on my own understanding (Proverbs 3:5). As I walk out into the deep, help me to fix my eyes firmly on You. Help me to stand on Your Word, Your living Word, to do the things You have called me to do, victoriously. In Jesus' name, AMEN!

CHAPTER 5

Faith Walk:
Genesis 37 & 39; 41:1-49
(Trusting God in the Process)

Summary: I wanted to take you through the process of Joseph's dream because this is the process of an entrepreneur. As you read it, you can feel the excitement, hurt, pain and frustration Joseph went through from the pit to the palace. Joseph had a vision that began at seventeen years old. And even after sharing it with his family, it didn't come to pass until he was almost forty years old.

Taken from the pit, from one household to another, along the way getting lied on and thrown in jail, and being forgotten. All that happened before getting to the palace.

Let's unpack this: As entrepreneurs God will give us a dream, vision, or a desire in our heart to do what He has called us to do. We get excited about it and run with it.

At times entrepreneurs will get the vision and start working towards it, finding ways to manifest what God has shown them. But you have to remember, the vision God has shown you, is the end result of the process. When God reveals the vision, you're at the beginning. So, there's a purging, a renewal mindset, a trust, leaning not on your own understanding that needs to happen. A deeper love for God is also needed for the journey, to carry you through the process to the end.

The next thing I want to discuss is the fact that Joseph's journey took him through a lot of different detours. Let's look at the meaning of detours: "The act of going or traveling to a place along a way that is different from the usual or planned way." The "usual" way of building your business may come from the world's point of view of doing whatever it takes, working hours upon hours and getting to the top by any means necessary. This is not realistic when you are a wife/husband, and a parent trying to build a business. God has a better and easier way of doing things.

Lastly, even though Joseph went from the pit to the palace, his dream did not manifest until years after he was in the palace.

His vision was: **Genesis 37: 6-7, 9**: *He said to them, "Hear this dream that I have dreamed: Behold, we were binding sheaves in the field, and behold, my sheaf arose and stood upright. And behold, your sheaves gathered around it and* *bowed down to my sheaf." Then he dreamed another dream and told it to his brothers and said, "Behold, I have dreamed another dream. Behold, the sun, the moon, and eleven stars were bowing down to me."*

The vision came to pass in **Genesis 42:6**, *"Now Joseph was governor over the land. He was the one who sold to all the people of the land. And Joseph's brothers came and bowed themselves before him with their faces to the ground."*

From the time he was 17 years old to about 40+, was when the vision came to pass. Along the journey, he was tested, he "practiced" his gift (dream interpreting) and was healed along the way. The hurt of feeling like an outsider in your family and being sold as a slave is hurtful. God had to heal Joseph's heart in the process of doing what he was called and purposed to do (Genesis 50:15-21).

Your calling is unique and only God has the blueprint for the success of your life. Following after other people who may be in the same boat, is the guaranteed way to disaster in all areas of your life.

Action Step: The way God takes you through the process in your journey will be different for someone else. Trust that God has a good plan for you (Jer. 29:11). Actively believe what He has spoken to you. Pray and ask God to see if the module that you have lines up with His. And the steps you have listed, are the ones He wants you to take to build your business.

Notes: In this section, write and talk with God about the steps you believe he's taking you through. If your business is a direct selling business and you have a plan in place to build your business, talk to God and ask Him if this is the way He wants you to go with your business. As you write and share what's in your heart, God may reveal to you the plan He has for your business.

_____

_____

_____

_____

_____

_____

_____

_____

S.M.A.R.T. Goals For Christian Entrepreneurs

_____

_____

_____

_____

_____

_____

_____

_____

_____

_____

_____

_____

_____

_____

_____

_____

_____

_____

_____

_____

_____

_____

_____

_____

_____

_____

_____

_____

_____

_____

_____

_____

_____

_____

S.M.A.R.T. Goals For Christian Entrepreneurs

_____

_____

_____

_____

_____

_____

_____

_____

_____

_____

_____

_____

_____

_____

_____

_____

Prayer: Lord, help me to stay the course no matter what happens along the way. Help me to firmly fix my eyes on you and not be moved by what's going on around me. Help me to truly walk by faith and not by sight. In Jesus' name, AMEN!

Next is a step by step process to achieve success in all areas of your life...

Chapter 6

S.M.A.R.T. GOALS
*The Practical Guide to Godly Success
in All Areas of Your Life*

S.M.A.R.T. stands for Specific, Measurable, Achieving, Realistic and Timely. This is what every small business/entrepreneur uses to make their business vision a reality. By setting these goals and achieving them, you can be successful in business.

Before we get started on S.M.A.R.T. goals for a Christian entrepreneur, we have to first define what success means to you. Are you working your business to provide for your family? Get famous? Have loads of money? Or do you want power? IF you answered yes to any of these questions, you may or may not be successful. If you do become successful, it will come at a great cost.

What is my definition of success? As God was working on my heart, I've learned that the definition for success is found in the bible, in **John 17:4**, "I glorified you on earth by completing down to the last detail what you assigned me to do" (Message Bible). Because we are God's own handiwork, we were created to do the works which God predestined (planned beforehand) for us to do, whether in business, marriage, raising our children, etc.

God has a plan and a work for us to do. So, in completing those plans and the work He called us to, I call it being successful, when we actually do it.

So, instead of following what everyone else thinks success is, we should be walking in faith, trusting that He has a better plan for us (Jeremiah 29:11). And by following these **S.M.A.R.T. goals**, I guarantee success in ministry, family life, business, and in all areas of life.

God uses us to accomplish His purpose on earth. Let me share with you another set of S.M.A.R.T. goals that God has given me to help you become effective in achieving the goals God has for your business.

S.M.A.R.T. goals for the Christian entrepreneur
S-Seek, **M**-Meditate, **A**-Armor, **R**-Run, **T**-Transformation.

Keys to being successful in life, business and in ministry, God's way!

<u>S-Seek: (Matthew 6:33) – Seek Him for the Answers</u>

But seek (aim at and strive after) first of all His kingdom and His righteousness (His way of doing and being right), and then all these things taken together will be given you besides. (Amplified Bible)

NOTE: You must seek God for your marriage, family life, ministry, business, and in all areas of your life so you can see His way of doing things, so you can be successful. This is a VERY important step as a Christian entrepreneur. Seeking God's direction, HIS way of doing things, in order to achieve the things God desires for your life.

When I first started my business, I felt God leading me in my heart to start a business. At the time, I didn't know what, when, where, or even how to start. I was very excited because I've always wanted to be an entrepreneur but never thought I would be starting from the ground up. I asked God what He wanted me to do, and He told me massage candles. Later on, it turned to hair and skin care products, along with the candles. Then He began to teach me about aromatherapy.

Find Him for the answer!

There was a time when I was seeking God for the next step for Silk Spa Creations, and I came across an opportunity to host an event called, "The Loc Appreciation Day Event." It's an event that happens all over the world, in places like Nigeria, London, Chicago, Atlanta, and New York (just to name a few), but there wasn't an event for San Diego, California. I was excited to be able to introduce this event to my area, but my husband and I were going through a very rough time in our finances and I didn't want to put another strain on our household. The other factors that I had to consider was the fact that I hardly knew anyone in the area and I had no idea on how to put an event together.

I not only prayed and sought God in scripture, but I also sought Godly advice and asked spiritual advisors to pray for me. During this time, God had pressed it upon my heart to not focus on the numbers, but to just put my heart into the event. I just needed to make sure that people experienced a quality event, and leave the rest of it up to God. After that I felt a fire in my heart to give it my best and once I stepped out, and depended on God, EVERY single detail had been worked out!

People not only came to the event, but I had the opportunity to meet the event planner for the company, Dr. Bonners Soap. We talked and he was happy to send their samples and products for the event giveaways. Taliah Waajid, a natural hair product company, sent bags with their samples as well. So many companies supported the event and there was even a reporter from the school university who came and did a piece on the event. I was just in awe at how much God had done. He worked it all out for me! He moved on my behalf because I sought Him first. I didn't want to make a move without Him and that pleased Him.

I'm sharing my story as a testament that God cares about every area of your life. **Seek Him for the answers and He will tell you**, be obedient and wait on God.

Note: Share what God is speaking to you about your business. **(Journal area)**

_____

_____

_____

_____

_____

_____

_____

_____

_____

_____

_____

_____

_____

_____

_____

_____

_____

_____

_____

_____

_____

_____

_____

_____

_____

_____

_____

_____

_____

_____

_____

_____

_____

_____

_____

_____

_____

_____

_____

_____

_____

_____

M-Meditate: (Joshua 1:8) – What's in Your Heart?

This Book of the Law shall not depart out of your mouth, but you shall meditate on it day and night, that you may observe and do according to all that is written in it. For then you shall make your way prosperous, and then you shall deal wisely and have good success. (Amplified Bible)

NOTE: Mediating on the word of God can help you stay focus on the purpose and plans God has for you, so you can make a difference in someone's life. When you make the decision to live God's way (kingdom living), you begin to change other people's lives naturally. When you have a deep, intimate relationship with God, it can reflect into the world, and in your everyday life.

What's in your heart?

Meditating on God's word can show us the state of mind our heart is in. During the journey of living out your vision or dream, God will use it to reveal what is in your heart that needs to change to prepare you for the manifested vision.

For me, this process has led me to know that when things get hard, I tend to quit, drop the ball and walk away. I can't be moved by everything that comes to challenge me, to quit in the middle of the battle (1 Corinthians 16:13), but that I must stand firm. When you quit in the heat, you hold back your blessings.

Remember: DON'T QUIT! I will discuss this more, later on in the chapter.

<u>**Note:**</u> Share what God is speaking to you about your business. **(Journal area)**

_____

_____

_____

_____

_____

_____

_____

_____

_____

_____

_____

_____

_____

S.M.A.R.T. Goals For Christian Entrepreneurs

S.M.A.R.T. Goals For Christian Entrepreneurs

A-Armor: (Ephesians 6:11-13) – Staying Equipped for Success

Put on God's whole armor [the armor of a heavy-armed soldier which God supplies], that you may be able successfully to stand up against [all] the strategies and the deceits of the devil.

For we are not wrestling with flesh and blood [contending only with physical opponents], but against the despotisms, against the powers, against [the master spirits who are] the world rulers of this present darkness, against the spirit forces of wickedness in the heavenly (supernatural) sphere.

Therefore put on God's complete armor, that you may be able to resist and stand your ground on the evil day [of danger], and, having done all [the crisis demands], to stand [firmly in your place] (Amplified Bible).

NOTE: Seeking first the kingdom is spiritual and the way God does things is spiritual. So, that means we have to always be in prayer, reading the bible, mediating on the word of God and being led by the spirit. These are important spiritual keys in succeeding in business, marriage, family life, etc.

Wearing God's armor is a business strategy. This means: "A method or plan chosen to bring about a desired future."

God desires to prosper you in all areas of your life.

<u>3 John 1:2</u>, "I pray for good fortune in everything you do, and for your good health—that your everyday affairs prosper, as well as your soul!" (Message Bible)

The Greek word for **"prosper"** is *euodoo* (yoo-od-o'-o) which means, *"To have a successful journey through life."*

Trust the process God is taking you through, because HE wants you to succeed more than you do!

<u>Note:</u> Share what God is speaking to you about your business. **(Journal area)**

_____

_____

_____

_____

_____

_____

_____

_____

_____

_____

_____

_____

_____

_____

_____

_____

_____

_____

_____

_____

_____

_____

_____

_____

_____

_____

R- Run: (Hebrews 12:1) – Run and Press Towards the Goal to Win the Prize

Therefore then, since we are surrounded by so great a cloud of witnesses [who have borne testimony to the Truth], let us strip off and throw aside every encumbrance (unnecessary weight) and that sin which so readily (deftly and cleverly) clings to and entangles us, and let us run with patient endurance and steady and active persistence the appointed course of the race that is set before us. (Amplified Bible)

NOTE: To persevere is staying in the race no matter what the obstacle. As a Christian entrepreneur, you're built as a soldier to endure. Running with endurance is very important because life happens and it can cause you to sometimes press through a little harder at times. I made the mistake of letting go of my business. I dropped the ball, a few years ago, because I became discouraged, lost, and stressed. The pressure of juggling multiple things at once caused me to lose out on helping women and missing out on the blessings that God had in store for me. ***Philippians 3:14***, "I press on toward the goal to win the prize for which God has called me..." We are built to endure the rough times.

I run to press toward the goal to win the

prize. The goal is to do what God has called me to do. The prize is seeing lives changed for the better, having a blessed family and business, and leaving behind a Godly legacy.

"Don't Quit!"

When things go wrong, as they sometimes will,
When the roads you're trudging seem all uphill,
When the funds are low and debts are high,
And you want to smile but you have to sigh,
When care is pressing you down quite a bit
 Rest if you must, but don't you quit.

For life is queer with its twists and turns,
As every one of us sometimes learns,
And many a failure runs about,
When he might have won had he stuck it out.
Don't give up though the pace seems slow,
You may succeed with another blow.

Often the goal is nearer than,
It seems to a faint and faltering man,
Often the struggler has given up,
When he might have captured the victor's cup;
And he learned too late when the night came down,
How close he was to the golden crown.

Success is just failure turned inside out,
The silver tint of the clouds of doubt,
And you never can tell how close you are,
It may be near when it seem so far.
So stick to the fight when you're hardest hit,
It's when things seem worst that you must not quit!

By: Author Unknown

Note: Share what God is speaking to you about your business. **(Journal area)**

_____

_____

_____

_____

_____

_____

_____

_____

_____

_____

_____

_____

_____

_____

_____

_____

_____

_____

_____

_____

_____

_____

_____

_____

_____

_____

_____

_____

S.M.A.R.T. Goals For Christian Entrepreneurs

_____

_____

_____

_____

_____

_____

_____

_____

_____

_____

_____

_____

_____

_____

_____

_____

_____

_____

_____

_____

_____

_____

_____

_____

_____

_____

_____

_____

_____

_____

_____

_____

_____

_____

_____

T-Transformation: (Romans 12:2) – The Heart Transplant

Do not be conformed to this world (this age), [fashioned after and adapted to its external, superficial customs], but be transformed (changed) by the [entire] renewal of your mind [by its new ideals and its new attitude], so that you may prove [for yourselves] what is the good and acceptable and perfect will of God, even the thing which is good and acceptable and perfect [in His sight for you]. (Amplified Bible)

Create in me a clean heart

(Psalm 51:10)
"Create in me a clean heart and renew a right spirit within me."

NOTE: God is more concerned with our heart than putting money in our pocket or bank account. It's important that our heart and mindset is in line with what He is doing, the way He thinks and does things. It's not easy and it takes a lot of prayer, seeking God's face, and FAITH!

The transformation God does in us, is to change our heart. He takes the things that are not like Him that is inside of us, out, and makes us more like Him. During the transformation, He is getting us prepared for the visions and dreams that He has placed in us. And along the way, He is healing us from past hurts, pains and anything else that may be a hindrance to what God is trying to do in our lives and others as well.

The transformation God has done in my heart has made such an impact in my life. It is one of the MAIN reasons I am writing this book. My desire is to be God's instrument in my marriage, my household and in the marketplace. I want to tell others of the night and day difference God has done in my life. He turned this nothing into something, from being rejected to being accepted (1 peter 2:9). I will leave a Godly legacy for my children to model after so that they can learn from my mistakes and do bigger and better things for God's kingdom.

Note: Share what God is speaking to you about your business. **(Journal area)**

_____

_____

_____

_____

_____

_____

_____

_____

_____

_____

_____

_____

_____

_____

_____

_____

_____

_____

_____

_____

_____

_____

_____

_____

_____

_____

_____

_____

_____

_____

_____

_____

_____

_____

_____

_____

_____

_____

_____

_____

_____

_____

_____

_____

_____

_____

_____

_____

_____

_____

_____

_____

_____

_____

_____

_____

_____

_____

Conclusion:

I pray this book filled with my testimonies, encouraging words and the Word of God will help catapult your life and heart's desires to Go BIG for the KINGDOM of God or Go HOME. God desires for you to have and enjoy life in abundance, to the full, and till it overflows, so that the next generation can go and experience even bigger and better things in life. So they, as well, can pass it on and so on. Your God-sized dream is not about you, it's about HIS PLAN and HIS way of doing things to not only bless you but others around you.

The message in this book and my speech was not written with wise and persuasive words. But I relied only on the power of the Holy Spirit. I wrote this way so that your faith might not rest on men's wisdom (**S.M.A.R.T.** goals) but on the power of God (the Word of God). ***1 Corinthians 2:4-5*** (Amplified Version)

I've learned that success is not a destination but it's a process. The process of your heart constantly changing towards His heart. I've also realized that it wasn't my job to figure ANYTHING out. Because His ways are not my ways and my thoughts are not His thoughts (***Isaiah 55:8-9***), and that God is the one that takes care of the details. It's just my job to be obedient to His word.

I will end with this quote that was sent to me from a friend. It was a great encouragement to me, in a time, when I felt so lost and was trying to figure everything out.

"You are the only you we have. That means your God-sized dream either happens through you or not at all."

God bless you in your endeavors…

Scriptures to meditate on and use for your entrepreneurship journey to motivate and encourage you along the way.

Isaiah 55:8-9

"For my thoughts are not your thoughts, neither are your ways my ways, declares the LORD. For as the heavens are higher than the earth, so are my ways higher than your ways and my thoughts than your thoughts."

Psalm 51:10

"Create in me a clean heart, O God, and renew a right spirit within me."

John 10:10(AMP)

"The thief comes only in order to steal and kill and destroy. I came that they may have *and* enjoy life, and have it in abundance (to the full, till it overflows)."

Romans 12:2(AMP)

"Do not be conformed to this world (this age), [fashioned after and adapted to its external, superficial customs], but be transformed (changed) by the [entire] renewal of your mind [by its new ideals and its new attitude], so that you may prove [for yourselves] what is the good and acceptable and perfect will of God, *even the* thing which is good and acceptable and perfect [in His sight for you]."

Philippians 3:14
"I press on toward the goal for the prize of the upward call of God in Christ Jesus."

Hebrews 12:1(AMP)
"Therefore then, since we are surrounded by so great a cloud of witnesses [who have borne testimony to the Truth], let us strip off *and* throw aside every encumbrance (unnecessary weight) and that sin which so readily (deftly and cleverly) clings to *and* entangles us, and let us run with patient endurance *and* steady *and* active persistence the appointed course of the race that is set before us."

3 John 1:2(Message Bible)
"I pray for good fortune in everything you do, and for your good health—that your everyday affairs prosper, as well as your soul!"

Ephesians 6:11-13(AMP)
"Put on God's whole armor [the armor of a heavy-armed soldier which God supplies], that you may be able successfully to stand up against [all] the strategies *and* the deceits of the devil.
For we are not wrestling with flesh and blood [contending only with physical opponents], but

against the despotisms, against the powers, against [the master spirits who are] the world rulers of this present darkness, against the spirit forces of wickedness in the heavenly (supernatural) sphere. Therefore put on God's complete armor, that you may be able to resist *and* stand your ground on the evil day [of danger], and, having done all [the crisis demands], to stand [firmly in your place]."

1 Corinthians 16:13
"Be watchful, stand firm in the faith, act like men, be strong."

Matthew 6:33(AMP)
"But seek (aim at and strive after) first of all His kingdom and His righteousness (His way of doing and being right), and then all these things taken together will be given you besides."

John 17:4(Message Bible)
"I glorified you on earth by completing down to the last detail what you assigned me to do."

Jeremiah 29:11
"For I know the plans I have for you, declares the LORD, plans for welfare and not for evil, to give you a future and a hope."

Mark 9:24

"Immediately the father of the child cried out and said, "I believe; help my unbelief!"

Proverbs 3:1-12

"My son, do not forget my teaching,
 but let your heart keep my commandments,
[2] for length of days and years of life
 and peace they will add to you.
[3] Let not steadfast love and faithfulness forsake you; bind them around your neck;
 write them on the tablet of your heart.
[4] So you will find favor and good success
 in the sight of God and man.
[5] Trust in the LORD with all your heart,
 and do not lean on your own understanding.
[6] In all your ways acknowledge him,
 and he will make straight your paths.
[7] Be not wise in your own eyes;
 fear the LORD, and turn away from evil.
[8] It will be healing to your flesh
 and refreshment to your bones.
[9] Honor the LORD with your wealth
 and with the firstfruits of all your produce;
[10] then your barns will be filled with plenty,
 and your vats will be bursting with wine.
[11] My son, do not despise the LORD's discipline
 or be weary of his reproof,
[12] for the LORD reproves him whom he loves,
 as a father the son in whom he delights."

Psalms 139:1-18, 23-24

O LORD, you have searched me and known me!

[2] You know when I sit down and when I rise up;
you discern my thoughts from afar.

[3] You search out my path and my lying down
and are acquainted with all my ways.

[4] Even before a word is on my tongue,
behold, O LORD, you know it altogether.

[5] You hem me in, behind and before,
and lay your hand upon me.

[6] Such knowledge is too wonderful for me;
it is high; I cannot attain it.

[7] Where shall I go from your Spirit?
Or where shall I flee from your presence?

[8] If I ascend to heaven, you are there!
If I make my bed in Sheol, you are there!

[9] If I take the wings of the morning
and dwell in the uttermost parts of the sea,

[10] even there your hand shall lead me,
and your right hand shall hold me.

[11] If I say, "Surely the darkness shall cover me,
and the light about me be night,"

[12] even the darkness is not dark to you;
the night is bright as the day,
for darkness is as light with you.

[13] For you formed my inward parts;
you knitted me together in my mother's womb.

[14] I praise you, for I am fearfully and wonderfully made.
Wonderful are your works;

my soul knows it very well.

[15] My frame was not hidden from you,
when I was being made in secret,
intricately woven in the depths of the earth.

[16] Your eyes saw my unformed substance;
in your book were written, every one of them,
the days that were formed for me,
when as yet there was none of them.

[17] How precious to me are your thoughts, O God!
How vast is the sum of them!

[18] If I would count them, they are more than the sand.

I awake, and I am still with you.

23 Search me, O God, and know my heart!
Try me and know my thoughts!

[24] And see if there be any grievous way in me,
and lead me in the way everlasting!

2 Corinthians 5:7

"For we walk by faith, not by sight."

Matthew 6:10

"Your kingdom come, your will be done, on earth as it is in heaven."

Ephesians 2:10(AMP)

"For we are God's [own] handiwork (His workmanship), recreated in Christ Jesus, [born anew], that we may do those good works which God predestined (planned beforehand) for us [taking paths which He prepared ahead of time], that we should walk in them [living the good life which He prearranged and made ready for us to live]."

Matthew 11:28-30

"Come to me, all who labor and are heavy laden, and I will give you rest. 29 Take my yoke upon you, and learn from me, for I am gentle and lowly in heart, and you will find rest for your souls. 30 For my yoke is easy, and my burden is light."

Deuteronomy 31:6

"Be strong and courageous. Do not fear or be in dread of them, for it is the LORD your God who goes with you. He will not leave you or forsake you."

Genesis 37:1-36

Joseph's Dreams

"Jacob lived in the land of his father's sojourning's, in the land of Canaan. These are the generations of Jacob. Joseph, being seventeen years old, was pasturing the flock with his brothers. He was a boy with the sons of Bilhah and Zilpah, his father's wives. And Joseph brought a bad report of them to their father. 3

Now Israel loved Joseph more than any other of his sons, because he was the son of his old age. And he made him a robe of many colors. But when his brothers saw that their father loved him more than all his brothers, they hated him and could not speak peaceably to him. Now Joseph had a dream, and when he told it to his brothers they hated him even more. He said to them, "Hear this dream that I have dreamed: Behold, we were binding sheaves in the field, and behold, my sheaf arose and stood upright. And behold, your sheaves gathered around it and bowed down to my sheaf." His brothers said to him, "Are you indeed to reign over us? Or are you indeed to rule over us?" So they hated him even more for his dreams and for his words. Then he dreamed another dream and told it to his brothers and said, "Behold, I have dreamed another dream. Behold, the sun, the moon, and eleven stars were bowing down to me." But when he told it to his father and to his brothers, his father rebuked him and said to him, "What is this dream that you have dreamed? Shall I and your mother and your brothers indeed come to bow ourselves to the ground before you?" And his brothers were jealous of him, but his father kept the saying in mind.

Joseph Sold by His Brothers
Now his brothers went to pasture their father's

flock near Shechem. And Israel said to Joseph, "Are not your brothers pasturing the flock at Shechem? Come, I will send you to them." And he said to him, "Here I am." So he said to him, "Go now, see if it is well with your brothers and with the flock, and bring me word." So he sent him from the Valley of Hebron, and he came to Shechem. And a man found him wandering in the fields. And the man asked him, "What are you seeking?" "I am seeking my brothers," he said. "Tell me, please, where they are pasturing the flock." And the man said, "They have gone away, for I heard them say, 'Let us go to Dothan.'" So Joseph went after his brothers and found them at Dothan. They saw him from afar, and before he came near to them they conspired against him to kill him. They said to one another, "Here comes this dreamer. Come now, let us kill him and throw him into one of the pits. Then we will say that a fierce animal has devoured him, and we will see what will become of his dreams." But when Reuben heard it, he rescued him out of their hands, saying, "Let us not take his life." And Reuben said to them, "Shed no blood; throw him into this pit here in the wilderness, but do not lay a hand on him"—that he might rescue him out of their hand to restore him to his father. So when Joseph came to his brothers, they stripped him of his robe, the robe of many colors that he wore. And they took him and threw him into a pit. The pit was empty; there was no water in it. Then they sat down to eat. And looking up they saw a caravan of Ishmaelites coming from Gilead, with their camels bearing gum, balm, and myrrh, on their way to carry it down to Egypt. Then Judah said to his brothers, "What profit is it if we kill our brother and conceal his blood? Come, let us sell him to the Ishmaelites, and let not our hand be upon him, for he is our brother, our own flesh." And his brothers listened to him. Then Midianite traders passed by. And they drew Joseph up and lifted him out of the pit, and sold him to the Ishmaelites for twenty shekels of silver. They took Joseph to Egypt. When Reuben returned to the pit and saw that Joseph was not in the pit, he tore his clothes and returned to his brothers and said, "The boy is gone, and I, where shall I go?" Then they took Joseph's robe and slaughtered a goat and dipped the robe in the blood. And they sent the robe of many colors and brought it to their father and said, "This we have found; please identify whether it is your son's robe or not." And he identified it and said, "It is my son's robe. A fierce animal has devoured him. Joseph is without doubt torn to pieces." Then Jacob tore his garments and put sackcloth on his loins and mourned for his son many days. All his sons and all his daughters rose up to comfort him, but he refused to be comforted and said, "No, I shall go down to Sheol to my son, mourning." Thus his father wept for him. Meanwhile the Midianites had sold him in Egypt to Potiphar, an officer of Pharaoh, the captain of the guard.

Genesis 39

Joseph and Potiphar's Wife

"Now Joseph had been brought down to Egypt, and Potiphar, an officer of Pharaoh, the captain of the guard, an Egyptian, had bought him from the Ishmaelites who had brought him down there. The LORD was with Joseph, and he became a successful man, and he was in the house of his Egyptian master. His master saw that the LORD was with him and that the LORD caused all that he did to succeed in his hands. So Joseph found favor in his sight and attended him, and he made him overseer of his house and put him in charge of all that he had. From the time that he made him overseer in his house and over all that he had, the LORD blessed the Egyptian's house for Joseph's sake; the blessing of the LORD was on all that he had, in house and field. So he left all that he had in Joseph's charge, and because of him he had no concern about anything but the food he ate. Now Joseph was handsome in form and appearance. And after a time his master's wife cast her eyes on Joseph and said, "Lie with me." But he refused and said to his master's wife,

"Behold, because of me my master has no concern about anything in the house, and he has put everything that he has in my charge. He is not greater in this house than I am, nor has he kept back anything from me except you, because you are his wife. How then can I do this great wickedness and sin against God?" And as she spoke to Joseph day after day, he would not listen to her, to lie beside her or to be with her. But one day, when he went into the house to do his work and none of the men of the house was there in the house, she caught him by his garment, saying, "Lie with me." But he left his garment in her hand and fled and got out of the house. And as soon as she saw that he had left his garment in her hand and had fled out of the house, she called to the men of her household and said to them, "See, he has brought among us a Hebrew to laugh at us. He came in to me to lie with me, and I cried out with a loud voice. And as soon as he heard that I lifted up my voice and cried out, he left his garment beside me and fled and got out of the house." Then she laid up his garment by her until his master came home, and she told him the same story, saying, "The Hebrew servant, whom you have brought among us, came in to me to laugh at me. But as soon as I lifted up my voice and cried, he left his garment beside me and fled out of the house." As soon as his master heard the words that his wife spoke to him, "This is the way your servant treated me," his anger was kindled. And Joseph's master took him and put him into the prison, the place where the king's prisoners were confined, and he was there in prison. But the LORD was with Joseph and showed him steadfast love and gave him favor in the sight of the keeper of the prison. And the keeper of the prison put Joseph in charge of all the prisoners who were in the prison. Whatever was done there, he was the one who did it. The keeper of the prison paid no attention to anything that was in Joseph's charge, because the LORD was with him. And whatever he did, the LORD made it succeed.

Genesis 40

Joseph Interprets Two Prisoners' Dreams

"Some time after this, the cupbearer of the king of Egypt and his baker committed an offense against their lord the king of Egypt. And Pharaoh was angry with his two officers, the chief cupbearer and the chief baker, and he put them in custody in the house of the captain of the guard, in the prison where Joseph was confined. The captain of the guard appointed Joseph to be with them, and he attended them. They continued for some time in custody. And one night they both dreamed—the cupbearer and the baker of the king of Egypt, who were confined in the prison

—each his own dream, and each dream with its own interpretation. When Joseph came to them in the morning, he saw that they were troubled. So he asked Pharaoh's officers who were with him in custody in his master's house, "Why are your faces downcast today?" They said to him, "We have had dreams, and there is no one to interpret them." And Joseph said to them, "Do not interpretations belong to God? Please tell them to me." So the chief cupbearer told his dream to Joseph and said to him, "In my dream there was a vine before me, and on the vine there were three branches. As soon as it budded, its blossoms shot forth, and the clusters ripened into grapes. Pharaoh's cup was in my hand, and I took the grapes and pressed them into Pharaoh's cup and placed the cup in Pharaoh's hand." Then Joseph said to him, "This is its interpretation: the three branches are three days. In three days Pharaoh will lift up your head and restore you to your office, and you shall place Pharaoh's cup in his hand as formerly, when you were his cupbearer. Only remember me, when it is well with you, and please do me the kindness to mention me to Pharaoh, and so get me out of this house. For I was indeed stolen out of the land of the Hebrews, and here also I have done nothing that they should put me into the pit." When the chief baker saw that the interpretation was favorable, he said to Joseph, "I also had a dream:

there were three cake baskets on my head, and in the uppermost basket there were all sorts of baked food for Pharaoh, but the birds were eating it out of the basket on my head." And Joseph answered and said, "This is its interpretation: the three baskets are three days. In three days Pharaoh will lift up your head—from you!—and hang you on a tree. And the birds will eat the flesh from you." On the third day, which was Pharaoh's birthday, he made a feast for all his servants and lifted up the head of the chief cupbearer and the head of the chief baker among his servants. He restored the chief cupbearer to his position, and he placed the cup in Pharaoh's hand. But he hanged the chief baker, as Joseph had interpreted to them. Yet the chief cupbearer did not remember Joseph, but forgot him.

Genesis 41:1-49

Joseph Interprets Pharaoh's Dreams
"After two whole years, Pharaoh dreamed that he was standing by the Nile, and behold, there came up out of the Nile seven cows attractive and plump, and they fed in the reed grass. And behold, seven other cows, ugly and thin, came up out of the Nile after them, and stood by the other cows on the bank of the Nile. And the ugly, thin cows ate up the seven attractive, plump cows. And Pharaoh awoke. And he fell asleep and

dreamed a second time. And behold, seven ears of grain, plump and good, were growing on one stalk. And behold, after them sprouted seven ears, thin and blighted by the east wind. And the thin ears swallowed up the seven plump, full ears. And Pharaoh awoke, and behold, it was a dream. So in the morning his spirit was troubled, and he sent and called for all the magicians of Egypt and all its wise men. Pharaoh told them his dreams, but there was none who could interpret them to Pharaoh. Then the chief cupbearer said to Pharaoh, "I remember my offenses today. When Pharaoh was angry with his servants and put me and the chief baker in custody in the house of the captain of the guard, we dreamed on the same night, he and I, each having a dream with its own interpretation. A young Hebrew was there with us, a servant of the captain of the guard. When we told him, he interpreted our dreams to us, giving an interpretation to each man according to his dream. And as he interpreted to us, so it came about. I was restored to my office, and the baker was hanged." Then Pharaoh sent and called Joseph, and they quickly brought him out of the pit. And when he had shaved himself and changed his clothes, he came in before Pharaoh. And Pharaoh said to Joseph, "I have had a dream, and there is no one who can interpret it. I have heard it said of you that when you hear a dream you can interpret it." Joseph answered

Pharaoh, "It is not in me; God will give Pharaoh a favorable answer." Then Pharaoh said to Joseph, "Behold, in my dream I was standing on the banks of the Nile. Seven cows, plump and attractive, came up out of the Nile and fed in the reed grass. Seven other cows came up after them, poor and very ugly and thin, such as I had never seen in all the land of Egypt. And the thin, ugly cows ate up the first seven plump cows, but when they had eaten them no one would have known that they had eaten them, for they were still as ugly as at the beginning. Then I awoke. I also saw in my dream seven ears growing on one stalk, full and good. Seven ears, withered, thin, and blighted by the east wind, sprouted after them, and the thin ears swallowed up the seven good ears. And I told it to the magicians, but there was no one who could explain it to me." Then Joseph said to Pharaoh, "The dreams of Pharaoh are one; God has revealed to Pharaoh what he is about to do. The seven good cows are seven years, and the seven good ears are seven years; the dreams are one. The seven lean and ugly cows that came up after them are seven years, and the seven empty ears blighted by the east wind are also seven years of famine. It is as I told Pharaoh; God has shown to Pharaoh what he is about to do. There will come seven years of great plenty throughout all the land of Egypt, but after them there will arise seven years of famine, and all the plenty will be forgotten in the land of Egypt. The famine will consume the land, and the plenty will be unknown in the land by reason of the famine that will follow, for it will be very severe. And the doubling of Pharaoh's dream means that the thing is fixed by God, and God will shortly bring it about. Now therefore let Pharaoh select a discerning and wise man, and set him over the land of Egypt. Let Pharaoh proceed to appoint overseers over the land and take one-fifth of the produce of the land of Egypt during the seven plentiful years. And let them gather all the food of these good years that are coming and store up grain under the authority of Pharaoh for food in the cities, and let them keep it. That food shall be a reserve for the land against the seven years of famine that are to occur in the land of Egypt, so that the land may not perish through the famine."

Joseph Rises to Power
This proposal pleased Pharaoh and all his servants. And Pharaoh said to his servants, "Can we find a man like this, in whom is the Spirit of God?" Then Pharaoh said to Joseph, "Since God has shown you all this, there is none so discerning and wise as you are. You shall be over my house, and all my people shall order themselves as you command. Only as regards the throne will I be greater than you." And Pharaoh

said to Joseph, "See, I have set you over all the land of Egypt." Then Pharaoh took his signet ring from his hand and put it on Joseph's hand, and clothed him in garments of fine linen and put a gold chain about his neck. And he made him ride in his second chariot. And they called out before him, "Bow the knee!" Thus he set him over all the land of Egypt. Moreover, Pharaoh said to Joseph, "I am Pharaoh, and without your consent no one shall lift up hand or foot in all the land of Egypt." And Pharaoh called Joseph's name Zaphenath-paneah. And he gave him in marriage Asenath, the daughter of Potiphera priest of On. So Joseph went out over the land of Egypt. Joseph was thirty years old when he entered the service of Pharaoh king of Egypt. And Joseph went out from the presence of Pharaoh and went through all the land of Egypt. During the seven plentiful years the earth produced abundantly, and he gathered up all the food of these seven years, which occurred in the land of Egypt, and put the food in the cities. He put in every city the food from the fields around it. And Joseph stored up grain in great abundance, like the sand of the sea, until he ceased to measure it, for it could not be measured.

Genesis 50:15-21

God's Good Purposes

"When Joseph's brothers saw that their father was dead, they said, "It may be that Joseph will hate us and pay us back for all the evil that we did to him." So they sent a message to Joseph, saying, "Your father gave this command before he died: 'Say to Joseph, "Please forgive the transgression of your brothers and their sin, because they did evil to you."'" And now, please forgive the transgression of the servants of the God of your father." Joseph wept when they spoke to him. His brothers also came and fell down before him and said, "Behold, we are your servants." But Joseph said to them, "Do not fear, for am I in the place of God? As for you, you meant evil against me, but God meant it for good, to bring it about that many people should be kept alive, as they are today. So do not fear; I will provide for you and your little ones." Thus he comforted them and spoke kindly to them."

ABOUT THE AUTHOR

Trista Laborn is passionate about helping individuals begin the process of doing business and living life God's way.

She is a wife to Enel Laborn, who has been serving in the United States Marine Corps for over 15 years. A mother of 3 beautiful children, a blogger, author, speaker, entrepreneur and founder of Silk Spa Creations.

She has a degree in Business Management and Ministry where she helps women get back to loving themselves naturally with *divine skin care.*

Author's note:

If you have been blessed by this book, or if your life and/or business has been impacted in any way, I would LOVE to hear from you.

Email me at: tlaborn@hotmail.com. Or stop by my website, www.adrivenwife.com for more information about Silk Spa Creations or if you just need to be encouraged to continue the journey that God has placed before you. Thank you and God Bless!

Facebook: www.facebook.com/adrivenwife
Twitter: www.twitter.com/tlaborn
Instagram: www.instagram.com/tlaborn

www.ingramcontent.com/pod-product-compliance
Lightning Source LLC
Chambersburg PA
CBHW070941210326
41520CB00021B/7008